THE HOLOCAUST AS CULTURE

Imre Kertész

THE HOLOCAUST AS CULTURE

TRANSLATED BY THOMAS COOPER

LONDON NEW YORK CALCUTTA

Seagull Books, 2018

'Imre Kertész and the Post-Auschwitz Condition'
© Thomas Cooper, 2011

'A Conversation with Imre Kertész'
© Thomas Cooper, 2010

'A Holocaust mint kultúra' © Imre Kertész, 1992

English translation, 'The Holocaust as Culture'
© Thomas Cooper, 2011

ISBN   978 0 8574 2 580 5

British Library Cataloguing-in-Publication Data
A catalogue record for this book is available
from the British Library

Typeset in Scala by Seagull Books, Calcutta, India
Printed and bound by Hyam Enterprises, Calcutta, India

IMRE KERTÉSZ
AND THE POST-AUSCHWITZ CONDITION

Though it may be a bit bold to offer a single statement on the vast and unfinished body of Imre
Kertész's work, one might venture the assertion
that in his novels, novellas, short stories and essays
Kertész is always grappling with the problems of
remembrance and forgetting and the inadequacies
and risks of representation. His works of fiction can
be read as expressions of the scepticism regarding
the notion of authenticity in the narrative that is
arguably the signature of the postmodern. In his
contributions to what he characterizes as 'the
monument—still under construction—to the
Holocaust', Kertész reminds his reader that the
traumas of the Holocaust elude representation
partly because representation transforms memory
into artefact and substitutes form for experience.
He identifies Auschwitz (and he is, of course, not
alone in doing so) as a moment of complete
rupture in European culture, a moment after which
the narrative models of the past are no longer available, at least not without the recognition of

Auschwitz as a refutation of the ethical teleologies that preceded it. His *oeuvre* raises the question, admittedly glib when put bluntly, as to whether, instead of a postmodern era, it might make sense to speak of a post-Auschwitz era, not simply to avoid the awkward terminology of the study of cultural history (a study often no less Eurocentric than the term post-Auschwitz might seem) but also because it is Auschwitz that seems to pose the greatest ethical challenge to representation itself. Can one represent experiences of trauma without assimilating them into interpretive frameworks and making them bearers of ideology? Can one create monuments to history without reducing history to an assortment of metonyms? Kertész's works can be read as attempts to do so, attempts at commemoration that resist the transformation of memory into myth and history into ideology.

Kertész's first collision with history as ideology came in 1973 with the submission of the manuscript of his novel *Sorstalanság*[1] to Magvető, one of

---

1 Imre Kertész, *Sorstalanság* (Budapest: Szépirodalmi, 1975). First translated into English as *Fateless* by Christopher C. Wilson and Katharina M. Wilson (Evanston, IL: Northwestern University Press, 1992) and then as *Fatelessness* by Tim Wilkinson (New York: Vintage, 2004). All subsequent quotations are from the latter.

the two leading publishing houses in Hungary at the time. The manuscript was rejected; and in a letter bearing the signature of György Kardos, the head of the publishing house, Kertész was reproached for failing to treat the subject matter with the solemnity it deserved as well as for displaying an offensive disrespect towards the victims of the deportations. The rejection of *Fatelessness* reveals a great deal about the ways in which the Holocaust was instrumentalized by the Communist regime in Hungary as a means of asserting its legitimacy.

Kertész was, in the early 1970s, essentially an unknown writer. Surviving his deportation to the concentration camps in 1944, he decided, following the Allied victory, to return to Hungary. There he completed high school and then worked briefly as a journalist. He was dismissed, however, from his position at the journal *Világosság* (Illumination) in 1950 for failing to adhere to the Party line. After two years of compulsory military service, he began to earn a living as an independent writer, collaborating on works for the theatre that, he later commented, he would always consider worthless. By the end of the 1950s, however, he decided to write about his experiences in the camps partly because, as he mentioned in his acceptance speech for the Nobel Prize in Literature in 2002, while attempting to recall his time in Auschwitz he found that little remained apart from 'a few muddled impressions, a few anecdotes'.[2]

Although Kertész has consistently maintained that *Fatelessness* is not autobiographical, the novel does bear a similarity to the story of his deportation in 1944 and his return to Budapest at the end of the War. György Köves the narrator is deported as a boy of 14 first to Auschwitz and then to Buchenwald and Zeitz. He falls ill and is kept alive by the other prisoners until, eventually, the camps are liberated by Allied forces. He returns to Budapest to find that his father, conscripted into a forced-labour unit a few months before his deportation, has perished in one of the camps. He converses briefly about his experiences with a journalist who then asks him why he repeatedly uses the word 'naturally' when speaking of things that are not natural, to which he can only reply that 'in a concentration camp, they *were* natural'.[3]

---

2 Imre Kertész, 'Heureka!' (2002). Available at http://www.nobel-prize.-org/nobel_prizes/literature/laureates/2002/kertesz-lecture-e.html

3 Kertész, *Fatelessness*, p. 247.

Fatelessness is distinctive in the literature of the Holocaust partly because of the narrator's failure to respond with shock or horror to the realities of the camps. He sees the German guards not as brutes or embodiments of evil but, rather, as humans responding to the exigencies of the moment and acting out of comprehensible motives. When he hears of the solicitude with which they lead prisoners to their deaths, allowing the children to sing and play football, and sees the picturesque settings of the gas chambers, surrounded by flower beds and groves of trees, he expresses no outrage but, rather, regards these details as understandably expedient parts of a well-thought-out plan. The whole apparatus of extermination reminds him of 'certain jokes, a kind of student prank', and he speculates on the process of working out the entire procedure:

> [P]eople would have had to meet to discuss this, put their heads together so to say, even if they were not exactly students but mature adults [. . .] One of them comes up with the gas, another immediately follows with the bathhouse, a third with the soap, then a fourth adds the flower beds, and so on. Some of the ideas may have provoked more prolonged discussion and amend-

ment, whereas others would have been immediately hailed with delight.[4]

He concludes his reflections with the remark that 'this was all too readily imaginable, at least as far as I was concerned.'[5] Even after weeks at the camp, György continues to regard the events as normal, noting, for instance, that 'naturally' he too suffered beatings at the hands of the guards, 'no more but also no less than normal, the average, the ordinary, like anyone'.[6] Of the guard who beats him when he drops a bag of cement he comments, 'his face bore what was almost a smile of satisfaction, [. . .] and from a certain perspective, I have to acknowledge, with good reason, for [. . .] I did manage to hold out [. . .] without dropping a single further bag, and that, [. . .] I would have to admit, proved him right.'[7]

Fatelessness was rejected by Magvető because it failed to conform to the prescribed opposition between National Socialism and Soviet Communism. As he mentions during our conversation, Kertész was expected to provide a narrative that fit

4 Ibid., p. 111.
5 Ibid.
6 Ibid., p. 168.
7 Ibid., p. 170.

the regime's 'story of occupation, persecution and liberation'. Far from offering a veiled parable of good and evil, the novel shies away from grandiose metaphor and metaphysical rumination and dwells instead on everyday life in the camps. The narrator's focus on incongruous or seemingly inconsequential details and his ability to find plausible explanations for the actions of the perpetrators undermined the narrative of the Communist regime in Hungary by presenting a vision of the Holocaust not as a closed chapter in a teleological narrative of progress but, rather, as the work of human hands and therefore something that could happen again.

Kertész wrote about the rejection of his manuscript in his novel *A kudarc*.[8] Often read as the second work in a trilogy beginning with *Fatelessness* and ending with the later *Kaddis a meg nem született gyerkekért*,[9] *The Fiasco* recounts the ultimately successful attempts by György Köves (also the name of

---

8 Imre Kertész, *A kudarc* (Budapest: Szépirodalmi, 1988). Translated by Tim Wilkinson as *The Fiasco* (New York: Melville House, 2011). As Wilkinson himself noted, 'The Failure' would have been a more fitting translation because the narrative recalls Samuel Beckett's play *Krapp's Last Tape* (1958) and Beckett's remark that 'to be an artist is to fail'.

9 Imre Kertész, *Kaddis a meg nem született gyerkekért* (Budapest: Magvető, 1990). Translated by Christopher C. Wilson and Katharina M. Wilson as *Kaddish for a Child not Born* (Evanston, IL:

the protagonist of *Fatelessness*) to find a publisher for his novel based on his experiences of the concentration camps and includes excerpts from the text of the letter signed by György Kardos[10] which begins with the reproach that the author's manner of 'artistic expression' is wholly inadequate to the 'horrific and shocking' subject matter. Citing passages from the manuscript of *Fatelessness*, the letter goes on to explain the readers' objections:

> We consider that your way of giving artistic expression to the material of your experiences does not come off, whereas the subject itself is horrific and shocking. The fact that it nevertheless fails to become a shattering experience for the reader hinges primarily to the main protagonist's, to put it mildly, odd reactions. While we find it understandable that the adolescent main protagonist does not immediately grasp what is happening round him (the call-up for forced labour,

Hydra Books, 1997) and later by Tim Wilkinson as *Kaddish for an Unborn Child* (London: Vintage, 2004).

10 Kertész has concluded that the letter was authored by György Kardos, but one cannot rule out the possibility that it was written by one of Kardos' underlings.

compulsory wearing of the yellow star, etc.), we think it inexplicable why, on arrival at the concentration camp, he sees the bald-shaven prisoners as 'suspect'. More passages in bad taste follow: 'Their faces did not exactly inspire confidence either: jug ears, prominent noses, sunken, beady eyes with a crafty gleam. Quite like Jews in every respect.'

It is also incredible that the spectacle of the crematoria arouses in him feelings of 'a sense of a certain joke, a kind of student jape', as he knows he is in an extermination camp and his being a Jew is a sufficient reason for him to be killed. His behaviour, his gauche comments repel and offend the reader.[11]

The letter concludes with a comment on the 'clumsy' and 'torturous' style and the recurrent use of allegedly awkward phrases such as 'naturally enough' and 'on the whole'.

---

11 Kertész, *The Fiasco*, pp. 56–7. There are inconsistencies in the translations, though both were by Wilkinson. The original letter cites the Hungarian text of *Fatelessness* but both the English translations contain small deviations, the use of the word 'jape', for instance, instead of 'prank'.

The accusations levelled against *Fatelessness* by the readers at Magvető exemplify the expectations of the regime regarding Holocaust narratives. The account of a survivor had to intone the voice of indignation and outrage and portray the machinery of deportation and extermination as evidence of the inhumanity of the perpetrators. Kertész commented on this in an interview in 1994, noting in particular the paradoxical proscription against writing about the Holocaust as a tragedy that had befallen European Jewry:

> In roughly 1975 the Jewry and Jewish identity were still taboo, and the camps were remembered first and foremost as prisons for communists. There was an 'expectation' that if someone wrote about the subject then he or she do so plaintively, as if lodging an appeal against nature, against civilization. Emphasis on uniqueness was mandatory, as was distancing, transformation into ideology and an obligatory bewilderment: how could what had taken place have taken place.[12]

---

12 Imre Kertész, 'A haláltudat mint vitalis erő' (The Sense of Death as a Vital Force). An interview by Szanto T. Gabor. *Szombat* 4

Fatelessness constituted a challenge to this sanctimonious pose. Kertész's use of the phrases 'naturally enough' and 'on the whole' was unpalatable, not because these phrases break the flow of otherwise elegant sentences but because they typify the narrator's tendency to see the events taking place round him as ordinary, or at least explicable. The regime sought portrayals of the Holocaust as something apocalyptic, portrayals that would fit well with the narrative of Communism as a kind of new beginning after a historical conflagration. *Fatelessness*, however, confronts the reader not so much with the barbarity of the crimes as it does with the perfunctory indifference with which they were committed. Mass executions, as the narrator of *The Fiasco* writes, are not a matter of an epic struggle between good and evil:

> [I]n some degree, over a certain time span and beyond a given number, [murder] is after all tiring, systematic, and harrowing work, whose daily continuity is not vouchsafed by the participants' likes or dislikes, bursts of ardour or onsets of disgust,

---

(1994): 35. Available at http://dia.pool.pim.hu/-html/muvek/ KERTESZ/kertesz00007/kertesz00021/kertesz00-021.html

enthusiasm or antipathy [. . .] but by organization, an assembly-line operation, a self-contained mechanism which does not permit so much as a moment's time to draw breath. In another respect, there can be no doubt about it, that is what put paid to tragic representation. Where would personalities who are grandiose, exceptional, and extraordinary even in their awfulness fit in? Richard III wagers that he will be evil; the mass murderers of a totalitarian regime, by contrast, take an oath on the common good.[13]

Fatelessness deflated the mystical ethos with which the regime had sought to invest Holocaust by depicting the perpetrators not as personifications of evil but, rather, as human beings responding to the demands and constraints of everyday life in the camps.

Kertész was also accused of being contemptuous towards the victims who he allegedly depicted in anti-Semitic terms and, indeed, the perceptions of the narrator of *Fatelessness* often seem shaped

---

13 Kertész, *Fatelessness*, p. 45.

by traditional Jewish stereotypes. One might explain his reactions, for instance his response, on arriving at Auschwitz, to the sight of the other prisoners ('jug ears, prominent noses, sunken, beady eyes with a crafty gleam. Quite like Jews in every respect'), as the internalization of prejudice by a boy socialized in a culture of anti-Semitism. These depictions, however, can be interpreted as another gesture of resistance on Kertész's part to the transformation of the Holocaust's events into ideological allegory. Kertész refuses to indulge in any simple oppositions. Perpetrator and victim act out of similar motives, and the willingness of the guards to follow the commands of their superiors is not distant from the ability of the prisoners to accept the conditions of the camp in order to survive. The novel yields no grand moral vision but illustrates instead the conclusion which Kertész later arrived at following the suppression of the 1956 Revolution in Hungary: 'The Kantian categorical imperative—ethics in general—is but the pliable handmaiden of self-preservation.'[14]

If the publication history of *Fatelessness* offers an illustration of the ways in which literary and

---

14 Kertész, 'Heureka!'

historical narrative was subjugated to ideology in Communist Hungary, it sidesteps the larger question of the possibilities and limits of representation after Auschwitz. As an interpretive method, the practice of tracing connections between contemporary exigencies and the reception of a work of art is ultimately a conventionally positivistic endeavour. Manipulations of history in the service of a regime offer reassuring examples of cause and effect, reassuring because they suggest that cause can be determined and agency identified, if not in the events of history then at least in the manners in which these events are fashioned into narrative.

The questions of representation after Auschwitz, however, involve the ethical implications of narrative itself as a displacement of experience. 'Discourse,' as Pierre Macherey writes, '[. . .] implies the temporary absence of the object of discourse; the object has been put to one side, banished into silence.'[15] Historians of the Holocaust have debated the appropriateness of traditional historical narrative with regard to the events

---

15 Pierre Macherey, *A Theory of Literary Production* (Geoffrey Wall trans.) (London and New York: Routledge & Kegan Paul, 2006), p. 67.

of the Holocaust, and some of the most prominent among them (one thinks of Raul Hilbert,
Hayden White, Berel Land and Saul Friedländer,
among others) have arrived at the conclusion that
conventional forms of representation are inadequate, a view perhaps most succinctly summa-
rized by Friedländer's contention that the task
of the historian in this particular case may well be
simply 'to produce the documentation; more
would be untenable or obscene'.[16]

Kertész shared this scepticism regarding the
validity of traditional narrative forms. As he
mentions in his Nobel Prize acceptance speech,
his writing was preoccupied with one question:
'What have I still got to do with literature? [. . .] we
must know that Auschwitz, in a certain sense at
least, suspended literature.'[17] Yet Kertész's scepticism goes beyond that of the historians. Friedländer's cautionary statement, however radical a
rejection of traditional historical narrative, does
allege the potential of historical discourse to recover
the past by tacitly affirming two fundamental

---

16 Saul Friedländer, 'The Historicization of National Socialism' in
Simone Gigliotti and Berel Lang eds, *The Holocaust: A Reader*
(Malden, MA, and Oxford: Blackwell Publishing, 2005), p. 297.

17 Kertész, 'Heureka!'

preconditions of historical writing: the possibility of an entirely referential discourse free of formal sublimations of meaning; and the authority of the present moment as a vantage point for evaluation. Kertész, though, does not share this self-assurance. His discourse is self-reflective, never stable, and always presented as a gesture of representation originating in the moment of composition rather than as an unmediated representation of a retrievable past.

Historical narratives derive their credibility from the assumed authority of the retrospective moment in which they are written. The work of Kertész, however, offers no self-assured perspective from which the past can be assessed and moral authority retrieved. This is perhaps most clearly illustrated by the differences between *Fatelessness* and the work of Jorge Semprun, also a Holocaust survivor and internationally acclaimed author. Semprun's first and perhaps best-known novel, *Le grand voyage*,[18] was published in Pál Réz's Hungarian translation in 1964. Kertész read

---

18 Jorge Semprun, *Le grand voyage* (Paris: Gallimard, 1963). Translated into English by Richard Seaver, it was published in the US as *The Long Voyage* (New York: Grove Press, 1964) and more recently in the UK as *The Cattle Truck* (London: Serif, 1993).

the novel and, as he commented in an interview, he regarded it as the exact opposite of what he sought to write. The chronology of Semprun's novel, a fictionalized version of the author's deportation to Buchenwald, is fractured. It jumps from the moment of narration (the train journey) backward in time to the narrator's participation in the French Resistance and then forward, to the liberation of the camp. The narrator, Gérard, recounts his deportation with a knowledge of the future, referring at times to things he will later come to know and evaluating the events of the present from the perspective of the wisdom he will gain. Assuming the full authority of his perspective, he interprets individuals and their deeds as emblematic of general truths expressed in parabolic terms. 'In the camps,' he asserts, 'man becomes that animal capable of stealing a mate's bread, of propelling him toward death. But in the camps man also becomes that invincible being capable of sharing his last cigarette butt, his last piece of bread, his last breath, to sustain his fellow man.'[19] Semprun returns to the events of the Holocaust in order to assimilate them into a

---

19 Semprun, *The Long Voyage*, p. 60.

fundamentally humanist worldview, a humanism that the Holocaust has not refuted but, rather, confirmed by provoking the implicitly shared (because unquestioned) outrage of narrator and reader.

Kertész adopted an entirely different approach. As he comments in his Nobel Prize acceptance speech, had he lived in the West he might well have written something resembling *Le grand voyage*: '[S]howier fiction [. . .] I might have tried to break up time in my novel, and narrate only the most powerful scenes.'[20] Living under another totalitarian system with its own compulsory routines, he sought instead to confront how the individual experiences the monotonies of everyday life. His protagonist, he notes, 'has to languish, poor boy, in the dreary trap of linearity, and cannot shake off the painful details. Instead of a spectacular series of great and tragic moments, he has to live through everything, which is oppressive and offers little variety, like life itself.'[21] This method, linearity, yielded an understanding of the processes of adjustment that, according to

---

20 Kertész, 'Heureka!'
21 Ibid.

Kertész, ultimately allowed the Holocaust to happen. Unlike the narrator of *Le grand voyage*, Kertész's protagonist has no grasp of what awaits him, and he cannot assess the events to which he bears witness from the privileged perspective of the future. When he characterizes the experience of being rounded up with other boys his age for deportation as 'slightly odd',[22] he is not adopting a deliberately ironic pose informed by foreknowledge of the camps. Rather, he is exhibiting precisely the ability to accept and adapt to changing circumstances that, in Kertész's view, made Auschwitz possible.

Kertész's discomfort with the authority of the retrospective moment implicit in traditional narrative finds further expression in his unease with language as a medium of representation. Here again the contrast with Semprun is illustrative. Semprun presents a stylistically consistent and coherent world in which the word is always adequate for the idea it embodies. Style is never interrogated, and the apparently self-evident meaning of abstractions such as 'destiny', 'freedom', 'historical essence', 'historical entity' and 'pure, fraternal

---

22 Kertész, *Fatelessness*, p. 40.

expression' is reinforced by the similarly implied suitability of conspicuously stylized discourse: 'I couldn't tell her that I was in the throes of dying, dying of hunger, far far from them, far from the wood fire and the words we were saying, in the snow in Thuringia amid the tall beeches through which the gusts of winter were blowing.'[23] Kertész, in contrast, writes not of ideas but events, and he is continuously troubled by the anxiety that his words distort rather than depict. 'It is impossible to write about the Holocaust,' he asserts in his essay 'A száműzött nyelv' ('The Exiled Tongue', 2001) but, as if bothered by the almost flippant smugness of this formula, which in itself trans- forms event into idea, he immediately adds: 'We could continue enumerating the paradoxical impossibilities ad infinitum. We could say it is impossible not to write about the Holocaust.'[24] As he begins to work on his novel, the narrator of *The Fiasco* grows increasingly uncertain of the value of his narrative as a mediation of his experiences:

---

23 Semprun, *The Long Voyage*, p. III.

24 See Imre Kertész, 'The Freedom of Self-Definition' in Horace Engdahl ed., *Witness Literature: Proceedings of the Nobel Centennial Symposium* (Singapore: World Scientific Publishing, 2002), p. 40.

> My work [. . .] actually consisted of nothing other than a systematic atrophying of my experiences in the interest of an artificial— or if you prefer, artistic—formula that on paper, and only on paper, I could judge as an equivalent of my experiences. But in order for me to write I had to look on my novel like every novel in general—as a formation, a work of art composed of abstract symbols [. . .] however, there was one thing that, perhaps naturally enough, I did not think of: we are never capable of interpreting for ourselves. *I* was taken to Auschwitz not by the train in the novel but by a real one.[25]

He reads an account of the murder of Dutch Jews in a rock quarry at Mauthausen according to which many of the prisoners chose to commit suicide by leaping from the sides of the pit rather than face death by overwork. The guards, disturbed by the sight of their tattered flesh dangling from quarry walls, tried to deter further attempts by brutally punishing anyone suspected of harbour-

---

25 Kertesz, *The Fiasco*, p. 73.

ing similar notions. 'These 340 deaths,' the narrator reflects, 'might rightly find a place among the
symbols of the human imagination—but on one
condition: only if they had not occurred.'[26] The
implication is that narrative can never represent
but only transform into allegory.

Kertész's anxieties regarding the inevitable
distortive potentials of representation call to mind
Theodor W. Adorno's famous dictum about the
barbarity of poetry after Auschwitz, a sentence
found in the concluding paragraph of his essay
'Cultural Criticism and Society' (1951). The affinity
of thought shared by the two writers, however, is
more profound. In his later *Negative Dialectics*,
Adorno revised this statement and made the underlying implication explicit:

> Perennial suffering has as much right to
> expression as a tortured man has to
> scream; hence it may have been wrong to
> say that after Auschwitz you could no
> longer write poems. But it is not wrong to
> raise the less cultural question whether
> after Auschwitz you can go on living [. . .]

26 Ibid., p. 47.

mere survival calls for the coldness, the
basic principle of bourgeois subjectivity,
without which there could have been no
Auschwitz.[27]

The coldness to which Adorno refers, the ability
to quieten the disturbed moral sense in order to
preserve fictions of social order, is exemplified in
Fatelessness by the narrator's ability to adapt
gradually but continuously to the world round
him. At the close of the novel he explains to some
of the surviving members of his family that they
too are implicated in what transpired for they had
been able and willing, at each stage, to make the
adjustments necessary to uphold the appearance
of normalcy. They had bid farewell to his father at
the train station, for instance, 'as if we had already
buried him'[28] and then squabbled over whether
the narrator should take the bus or the train to
Auschwitz, as if the question was relevant. This
appearance of normalcy, maintained through an
adherence to familiar routines, functions as an
alibi for self-preservation.

---

27 Theodor W. Adorno, *Negative Dialectics* (E. B. Ashton trans.)
(New York: Continuum, 1973), pp. 362–3.

28 Kertész, *Fatelessness*, p. 260.

With the gradual passing of the last generation of Holocaust survivors, questions of representation may become increasingly significant as
living memory yields entirely to commemoration,
as the Holocaust becomes nothing other than
the forms it has been and continues to be given
in culture. Arguably we live today amid a proliferation of Holocaust culture, a proliferation that
has included new appropriations of history in the
service of cultural exigencies of the present. In
today's parables of redemption, Auschwitz is cast
as the symptom of a deep psychological malady
of which Western culture, seemingly healthy for
centuries, had lived in denial. If we can find an
adequate form of communal atonement, these
narratives suggest, then we can heal this culture
and salvage the virtues of its traditions. One
thinks of Steven Spielberg's *Schindler's List* (1993),
a story of conversion and redemption through res-
cue that follows the Christian model with due ser-
vility. Roman Polanski's *The Pianist* (2002, based
on the autobiography of Władysław Szpilman),
the story of a Jewish pianist whose performance
almost moves a Nazi to tears, reasserts the notion
of a common humanity dear to the humanist tra-
dition. Rituals of remembrance have emerged that

similarly threaten to dilute whatever might be preserved of the memory of the Holocaust. Auschwitz itself has become one of the stops on a European grand tour that might well also include Versailles or the Uffizi.

As tempting as it may be to dismiss these narratives and rituals of commemoration as examples of an increasingly pervasive Holocaust kitsch, one should not be presumptuous. It would be pedantic and falsely naive to pretend to aspire to narrative forms that are resistant to any and all forms of sentimental interpretation. Nor need one dwell on the limits of our ability, as spectators, to understand the experiences of survivors. Were that the case, the consumption of any artefact, any attempt at commemoration, would be little more than an obligatory gesture of obeisance before a kind of monolith to an unknowable.

If it seems at times that we are surrounded by a profusion of Holocaust culture, this profusion need not be seen as surplus. Diversity of form forces questioning of form, and one approach to depiction does not supplant but merely qualifies another. *Fatelessness* constitutes a response to *Le grand voyage* (among other works), not a refutation.

New attempts at representation will not result in wholly adequate or authentic portrayals but, rather, will offer perspectives for comparative re-examination of the underlying assumptions and ideological motivations of other attempts. The work of Kertész freed the memory of the Holocaust from a rigid ideological mould, transforming it from mute emblematic museum piece to lived individual experience. If culture is to continue to function as the vessel of memory, it will do so through similar continuous interrogation of received versions of the past.

Thomas Cooper, 2011

A CONVERSATION WITH
IMRE KERTÉSZ

THOMAS COOPER. Let me begin by thanking you for setting aside time to talk about your work. I had the pleasure of teaching *Fatelessness* several years ago as part of a course on Hungarian literature at the University of North Carolina. For my students, and I confess for me, it was a Holocaust novel. But I recall you commented in 2003 that the book was as much about the Kádár system as it was about the Holocaust, and this comment became the subject of some debate. May I ask you to explain what you meant?

IMRE KERTÉSZ. First, I would never call *Fatelessness* a Holocaust novel because the Holocaust, or what people mean when they use that word, can't be put in a novel. I was writing about the camps, the experiences of the camps. I was born in 1929, so I was a child when I was deported. I began working on *Fatelessness* in the

1960s, and it was partly the Communist system under Kádár that gave me the push to try
to understand what I had lived through as a
child. I wanted to write about the experiences
of the camps, nothing but the events, but I was
also interested in the specific way in which the
individual is deprived of his or her fate in a
dictatorship. This was an aspect of dictatorship
that concerned me, and the Kádár regime was
a dictatorship. Living in the Kádár regime
helped me understand the workings of a dictatorship, and this in turn helped me understand my experiences in the camps. I'm not
saying Kádár was the same as Hitler but that
the dynamics of dictatorship were all there.

COOPER. It is one of the peculiarities of the publication history of *Fatelessness* that when you
completed the manuscript and you took it to
Magvető, they rejected it, even claimed it was
anti-Semitic.

KERTÉSZ. Yes, the old Magvető, they did.

COOPER. It remains a bit difficult for me to understand this. In what kind of ideological framework could *Fatelessness* be characterized as

anti-Semitic? How did the editors interpret the book?

KERTÉSZ. Well, look, I was 24 or maybe 25 when I began writing or, rather, when I realized that I had to write. I had to think about exactly how I wanted to approach writing, what I wanted to write and how I should work through my past. When I began writing *Fatelessness*, I wanted to get at the events as I had lived them and I wanted to avoid any sentimentality. But, at that time in Hungary, they either tried to hush up talk about the Holocaust or to treat it as a Jewish affair. Works dealing with the Holocaust were expected to be full of passionate outrage but there was no space in which one could retell the events and experiences.

COOPER. And *Fatelessness* did not meet these expectations?

KERTÉSZ. The narrator of *Fatelessness* is a young boy and I quickly realized that of course the language had to be that of a young boy, and this ended up playing an important role in shaping the narrative. It is not ideological. I wrote it as a kind of continuous recounting of events but in the language and from the perspective of a young boy. This came out well, because it had the effect of estranging me from the narrative a bit, the perspective became one of observation. I tried to put down the everyday experiences of the camp. It threw a kind of existential glance on the events, and this may have been surprising for some readers. It certainly didn't fit with the regime's mould. There is no stable system of values in the novel, everything is mocking, saturated with irony. The boy sees prisoners slipping out of line and fleeing as the police round them up and he thinks to himself, 'I'll be honest and respectful' even when one of the policemen encourages him to take advantage of the chance to flee. Of course, what is his honesty worth in Auschwitz?

COOPER. When I taught this novel at universities in the United States, my students were obviously familiar with other Holocaust narratives, usually Elis Wiesel's *Night* [1960] but others as well. They found *Fatelessness* troubling as a narrative because it seemed to consist of a fragmented series of events. It did not yield to any allegorical interpretation, as the title suggests, very unlike *Night*. For them, the passages at the close of the novel, in which the narrator writes of the joys of the camps, were difficult to reconcile with their knowledge of the Holocaust (which is, of course, entirely a product of other narratives). I would be curious to know why you considered it important, when you wrote the novel, to avoid allegory.

KERTÉSZ. Well, let's be honest, there are two kinds of Holocaust stories: positive and negative. I mean, there are Holocaust stories with happy endings. You think of Steven Spielberg in the United States, for instance. But people talk about the Holocaust and inhumanity . . . well . . . it was of course humans who were responsible, so I'm not sure it makes much sense to talk about inhumanity.

COOPER. The regime in Hungary has become infamous for the ways in which it instrumentalized the Holocaust. Did this have anything to do with the allegation that it was anti-Semitic?

KERTÉSZ. Yes, absolutely. About two years after I was awarded the Nobel Prize I was interviewed for *Élet és Irodalom* (Life and Literature) by a woman with the name of Eszter. I mentioned to her that I really began to understand the workings of total dictatorship under Kádár. Of course, Nazi tyranny and Auschwitz were horrors but, as I said, I was a child at the time. Under the dictatorship of Mátyás Rákosi, which was utterly brutal, one had a clear goal: to survive. But under Kádár our boats all ran aground; we were left stranded. I had time to look round and assess the machinery of a dictatorship, the ways in which the so-called soft dictatorship made people complicit. Because the machinery was all there we called it a soft dictatorship, but what does that mean anyway? I spoke about all this in the interview and you cannot imagine the outcry with which it was met. One critic said I should give back the Nobel Prize, because I hadn't won it so that I could soil the memory of the Kádár era. Some people remain nostalgic about the old system even today.

COOPER. In your acceptance speech you mentioned that one could not imagine any freedom greater than that enjoyed by a writer living in a relatively closed, weary, even decadent dictatorship.

KERTÉSZ. Yes, I was entirely unknown. I was lucky in this sense because I wrote as I pleased and no one gave a damn.

COOPER. In one of your essays you mentioned that unlike [Paul] Celan, [Tadeusz] Borowski, [Jean] Améry and Primo Levi . . .

KERTÉSZ. Borowski, Améry—I have always thought of them as spiritual siblings.

COOPER. But unlike them you lived in a culture in which all talk of freedom, catharsis, liberation, etc., was lip service to the regime and its official narratives. So you never had to endure the disappointments they suffered.

KERTÉSZ. Yes, I realized quite early on that if I wanted to be a writer and write what I wanted, not what was wanted of writers, then I shouldn't let anyone know I was writing, shouldn't let anyone know that some guy named Imre Kertész was sitting in his apartment working on a novel. I didn't want to be a part of the literary scene, you know, a writer submits the manuscript of a novella, then waits patiently to hear from the publisher. I decided that the novel I was writing was important to me, so I chose the worse of the two publishers. There were two leading publishers at the time for works of literature, Magvető and Szépirodalmi Könyvkiadó. I figured that Magvető was more likely to publish something jarring. But I didn't know the head of Magvető, a man named György Kardos. He was a high-ranking Party functionary. He had been part of military intelligence and served a prison sentence under Rákosi, but he found a niche for himself under Kádár. It's funny how censors and dictators seem to love literature but have the worst taste! Of course, in 1975, the regime in Hungary was trying to depict itself as more open than the dictatorships in the neighbouring countries, and it was , as we say, 'softer'. But when Kardos got my manuscript he stuck to the usual line. He wanted a book that brought him to tears, a kind of outcry against injustice. And in 1975 it was still taboo to talk about the persecution of the Jews by the Nazis—you were supposed to talk about the persecution of the Communists and Communist sympathizers. The regime al-

ways wanted something it could plug into its
story of occupation, persecution and liberation.
Of course, that's not what *Fatelessness* is. But I
left the manuscript with Magvető, gave it to a
secretary, then finally spoke to the chief editor.
I asked him what they'd thought of the novel.
He said he hadn't read it but I remember him
asking, 'Isn't it a bit bitter?' 'Well, yes,' I
replied, 'but the subject isn't exactly cheery.' Of
course, I was joking but two days later I got
back the manuscript with a letter of rejection
from Kardos in which he accused me of anti-
Semitism. How can you write about Jews at
Auschwitz so insolently, etc., etc. But I was
lucky. Usually Kardos would sign a contract for
a book, pay an advance and then sit on it for
years. When the contract ran out, he would
either return the manuscript to the author or
sign a new contract. It's a debilitating system.
It was my good fortune that they wanted nothing to do with the novel. I figured if one publisher had shown no interest then there was no
point in showing it to another. But a friend per-
suaded me to be more open, to wait until the
other house let me know its decision. So I sub-
mitted it to Szépirodalmi Könyvkiadó. Two of

their readers gave positive assessments and
they published it based on that alone. But it
didn't really draw much attention, either at the
publishers or among the public. Two or three
weeks after its publication I decided to buy a
few copies for my friends but I couldn't find it
anywhere. Of course, you have to know how
many copies were published, how many copies
the socialist system thought worth publishing—5,000! An American or European publisher would faint! But they printed 5,000
copies and I thought it was a fantastic success!
Then a friend suggested that I visit the huge
bookstore on Csont Street at Csepel Island. I
did so, and found copies of *Fatelessness* stacked
in towers, waiting to be turned into pulp! This
was the world of socialism in Hungary—nothing in it was real. Somehow the novel had
managed to slip through the cracks and be
published, but then nothing, it came to nothing. Then eight years later it was published
again. György Spiró—I'm sure you've heard of
him, he was a recipient of the Attila József
Prize—wrote an article on it in *Élet és Irodalom*.
I didn't know him at the time but his article
made it clear that members of the younger

generation were reading the novel and that copies of it were even being sold on the black market. Then, in 1985, it was published again. It gained more official recognition and drew some attention but still not much.

COOPER. It's interesting, partly because the book was not entirely unknown outside of Hungary. Éva Haldimann wrote about it in 1977, only two years after its publication by Szépirodalmi Könyvkiadó.

KERTÉSZ. Yes, she wrote articles about Hungarian literature in German periodicals. I did not know her then but later we began to correspond. Some of our letters have been collected now and published.

COOPER. She was writing about the Hungarian novel which hadn't been translated at the time.

KERTÉSZ. Yes, copies were smuggled out of the country and read abroad, which is funny since I myself had trouble getting copies at first. But the novel was read by a small circle of intellectuals who devoured it without ever actually writing about it. Haldimann was the exception. But, you know, if you have something to write then you write it—you don't think about your audience.

COOPER. From time to time, actually not infrequently, one comes across comparisons. Auschwitz and the Holocaust are used as a kind of measuring stick to assess the horrors of some other tragedy or outrage of history. Parallels have been drawn between the deportation and massacre of Armenians in the Ottoman Empire in the First World War but also, more recently, in descriptions of events of the wars in Bosnia. How do you respond to this use of Auschwitz as a sort of quintessence of evil?

KERTÉSZ. I don't think these comparisons are justified or useful. When you make comparisons like this, you remove the events from their context. How does this further our understanding? I still think Auschwitz is unique in history. The construction of gas chambers, the whole complex machinery of extermination. Of course, appalling massacres had been carried out before but deporting and slaughtering a civilian population, a population whose labour was an asset to the German army—it's unique in history, even in Jewish history which was full of pogroms. But, as [Raul] Hilberg noted, everything that happened to European Jews in the twentieth century, all the persecution, the yellow star and the ghettoes, the seizure of property, there was a historical precedent for it all. It had all happened in some form or the other. Auschwitz was the only exception.

COOPER. In *K. dosszié,*[1] you cite Giorgio Agamben and his contention that the word Holocaust arises from the unconscious demand to justify a death that is *sine causa*. Could *Fatelessness* be read as a similar rejection of this demand? I'm thinking of the narrator's hesitation to use any abstractions to describe his experiences in the camps, his refusal to describe the camps as hell because, as he says, he has no idea what hell is like.

KERTÉSZ. Look, in the end these are just words. Holocaust, Shoah, I use them too because it's unavoidable. But words are just a matter of consensus. Everyone says Auschwitz for Holocaust or Holocaust for Auschwitz. You know,

---

1 Imre Kertész, *K. dosszié* (Budapest: Magvető, 2006).

the historian, Raul Hilberg, he's passed away now, but his book was simply entitled *The Destruction of the European Jews* (1981). Maybe this is what we should say, maybe every time we speak about the Holocaust we should just say 'the destruction of the European Jews'. Maybe we could get rid of the Spielberg interpretations of the Holocaust, the 'we survived' interpretations, the 'we should be happy, the Jewish people survived, we have many dead but in the end the Jewish people survived' interpretations. I don't even know what this 'Jewish people' is, to be honest, but perhaps we shouldn't raise that question. It's a complicated one.

COOPER. If you'll forgive me for bringing up the question anyway: Does it make sense in your case to speak of Judaism without mention of Auschwitz?

KERTÉSZ. In my case, no. My Jewishness is shaped by the Holocaust. I do not speak Hebrew, I did not have a religious education or upbringing, I am not familiar with Jewish philosophy, I do not know the Kabbalah. I would use Isaac Deutscher's term to describe myself: I am a non-Jewish Jew. I am not religious, I never was. Religion has never meant anything to me. I once heard someone put it perfectly, 'God has no religion.' He was a Calvinist pastor, speaking as part of his regular service. I can't remember exactly when I heard it but this is my view too. Although the thought of Israel is still very tender, fragile, to me, and I express my solidarity whenever I have the opportunity. But it is not my home or homeland.

COOPER. You commented once that the word Holocaust refers to those who perished, in other words those who were burnt, and forgets those who survived.

KERTÉSZ. Yes, survival was the exception, a flaw in the Nazi machinery, as Améry wrote. The survivor is the accident, or the mistake, that which needs explanation. Survival seems unimaginable but actually it is the camps that should seem unimaginable. You know, this was one of the strange things about my memories of Buchenwald. In the middle of the camp was a hospital where they tended to the ailing. How was this possible? And then you realize the question is: How was the camp possible?

COOPER. Améry wrote about his fear that, with the passing of the last generation of survivors, the memory of the Holocaust would pass as well. Do you share this fear?

KERTÉSZ. I spoke about Améry during my presentation at the University of Vienna in 1992. That was when I wrote the essay 'A holocaust mint kulturá' ('The Holocaust as Culture'). Essentially I meant to set forth my view that if the memory of the Holocaust is to remain then it will remain through culture, which is really the vessel of memory. Borowski also feared that the memory of Auschwitz would fade. But I think they were wrong. Auschwitz casts a long shadow over European civilization and is still the vital question of our culture. I spoke about this as part of my presentation, and the audience, mostly members of the younger generation, seemed interested. And I began to think a bit about the nature of trauma and historical memory. The Holocaust was a trauma, but its expression was stifled for the generation that lived through it. There were these mute decades. Then the symptoms began to erupt in our culture, and the symptoms were what let us know that the trauma had occurred, and let us begin working through what had happened. Of course, in Eastern Europe the whole discussion was distorted by the system, by the official version of liberation, etc. Even today one can see significant differences in the way in which the Holocaust has been treated as historical memory in the East and in the West.

COOPER. From what perspective?

KERTÉSZ. Simply, that it has been given such thorough attention, in history, art, literature. It has become part of Western Europe's cultural past. The Holocaust is an absolute turning point in Europe's history, an event in the light of which will be seen everything that happened before and that will happen after. Chancellor Merkel, when she took office, said that the Holocaust was a part of the German Volk, the identity of the German Volk. And, of course, most of the historical scholarship on the Holocaust has been done in Germany. But the point is that it's not seen simply as an event of history but, rather, as an event that casts an entirely different light on all our ideas about ethics and morality.

COOPER. And you are suggesting that the Communist regime in Hungary played a role in stifling similar discussion?

KERTÉSZ. Absolutely, and they were quite candid about it too. The whole question of anti-Semitism was swept under the carpet during the Kádár regime. You couldn't be openly anti-Semitic, that wasn't tolerated, but it was all false. They used 'persecuted' instead of 'Jew'. It was risky to say 'Jew'. So, in a way, we became invisible. We were there as the victims of the persecution from which the Soviet Army had supposedly saved us but we couldn't be there as Jews.

COOPER. Did the Cold War alliances have any role in this?

KERTÉSZ. Yes, definitely. The basic stance of the government was 'It's fine to be Jewish in Hungary but only if you bear no sympathy for Israel.' It was just another kind of total assimilation. I could tell you a story about this. A man, prominent in the cultural life of Hungary, asked me for a manuscript. I ran into him at the theatre and he asked me if I was working on anything. I said I wasn't working on any novella or anything like that but I did have an essay that might interest him. 'More Holocaust stuff?' he asked. He was Jewish, and this was how he responded. The entire Jewish intelligentsia is so accustomed to this pressure to assimilate, to talk but to be quiet at the same time. You know, there was a *numerus clausus* in the interwar period, and society was much more openly anti-Semitic. Under Bethlen, the Jewish communities of Hungary renamed themselves Neologue. Only they knew exactly what they meant by this. At the very least it was as if they wanted to make it clear that they bore no affinities with Orthodox Jewry, with Jews in the eastern part of the country. And they showed their perfect willingness to assimilate, at least as much as they would be allowed to do so. Even to convert, though of course this meant nothing when deportations began. You know the poet Miklós Radnoti, he was a converted Catholic and always thought of himself as a Hungarian. He was sent to the camps, and then they shot him by the side of the road during a march to Germany. But the role of the Church in Hungary was different than in Germany. In Germany, the Catholic Church had little significance, and the Jewish question had nothing to do with the churches—it was entirely secular. In Hungary, the bishops had to vote on the Jewish laws, like the 1938 laws. This is something people should know. The parliament in Hungary had an upper house and a lower house, and the bishops sat in the former. And when the question came up in 1938 they voted in support of the Jewish laws. Of course they weren't voting to kill all the Jews, but they did vote to have them excluded from schools, to allow for the seizure of their property, etc. The Church in Hungary played a role in this.

Switzerland organizes a book fair every two years. I was invited once and, to my great surprise, the man representing the Hungarian Embassy—not officially, he had just come to the fair—gave a very eloquent speech about the Holocaust. We spoke, and it turned out that he was László Ravasz's nephew. He was deeply ashamed of the anti-Semitism of the Church in Hungary, and he was always working to-wards a greater knowledge of the events of the

Holocaust. But the point is that these people were there, they had to vote for or against these laws and they voted for them. The persecution of the Jews in Hungary was a bit different from the persecution of the Jews in Germany in this regard. In Germany, the government first took all power from the churches and then there was one-party rule.

COOPER. You have written in several of your essays that the meaning of the term Jew has changed since the Holocaust. Could the same be said of anti-Semitism? Is anti-Semitism also different after Auschwitz?

KERTÉSZ. Of course, entirely different. To be anti-Semitic after Auschwitz is to support Auschwitz. An anti-Semite today, knowing that something like Auschwitz is possible, denies it but not because he cares about whether or not it really occurred. Of course it did—that's not a question. He denies it in order to make it possible for it to happen again. Before Auschwitz there existed a sort of cultural anti-Semitism, like Richard Wagner's anti-Semitism. I am not convinced that Wagner would have approved of the Holocaust.

COOPER. What about Nietzsche? I know you translated Nietzsche, at a time when he was frowned
upon, to say the least, by the government.

KERTÉSZ. Oh yes, I am certain he would have been
the first person to be sent to the camps. The
very person whose ideas the Nazis claimed as
their own. Nietzsche was constantly questioning—they would have put him on the first
train! I am suspicious of all the explanations
that tie Hitler to Nietzsche or to Faust or to
Luther, for that matter. If we want to understand National Socialism then we need to understand the workings of a dictatorship in
which the individual was deprived of the ability
to decide and was forced to play a role in the
system. But this is not something peculiar to
German history. We speak of collective guilt,
the collective guilt of the German nation. But
Auschwitz is the collective crime of the entire
world, not just of the German nation. If we
think of the Holocaust as a war between
Germans and Jews then we will never understand it.

COOPER. Your interest in German literature is well
known, as are your translations from German

to Hungarian. I know, for example, that you have translated Elias Canetti.

KERTÉSZ. Yes, I have. A fascinating writer. I translated *Das Augenspiel* [1985].

COOPER. You've also translated [Hugo von] Hofmannsthal and [Joseph] Roth as well as Wittgenstein and Freud, which was a bit risky under Kádár. Was it some relief from the isolation of the Eastern Bloc to be able to read the writings of these authors?

KERTÉSZ. Absolutely. You have to understand that in my youth I could only read Marxist philosophy. And I grew terribly bored with it. Then, in the 1960s, Kant's *Critique of Judgement* was published in Hungarian translation and it opened a new path for me into the world of philosophy.

COOPER. Has literature in English, or American literature in particular, had any influence on your work?

KERTÉSZ. I recall a novel by an American author, Kurt Vonnegut, and I remember well the description of the bombing of Dresden, a kind of terror bombing against the civilian population, an answer to the bombing of London. The city burnt for hours and everyone above ground perished, a horrible thing. There is a German writer by the name of W. G. Sebald, he has a book called *Luftkrieg und Literatur*[2]— have you read it?

COOPER. No.

KERTÉSZ. I recommend it, it's a slender volume. He looks at how the bombing of Dresden is remembered, or actually almost forgotten, by the Germans, by the German historical memory. You know, the German nation is a complicated thing. Lots of people speak German outside Germany, and then there's the German state. So the question of identity is always there. But whenever this question comes up Auschwitz is always present, overwhelmingly so. I think Auschwitz prevented a generation of Germans from being able to talk about their own suffering in the War. Cicero says that if you don't learn what's happened since your birth, you remain a child.

---

2 W. G. Sebald, *Luftkrieg und Literatur: Mit einem Essay zu Alfred Andersch* (Munich: Carl Hanser Verlag, 1999). Translated by Anthea Bell as *On the Natural History of Destruction* (London: Hamish Hamilton, 2003).

COOPER. You have written about memory and the importance of writing as creating in the process of remembrance. What is the relationship between creation and remembrance in your works?

KERTÉSZ. Creation is a path to remembrance. When I started to write, my memories of the camps lay dormant. But as you start to create, to write, you bring them out of this obscurity. This is when they begin to seem absurd and you try to understand them, and as you do they pass into fiction. Many of the events that I wrote about in *Fatelessness* happened just as I recounted them but I still can't think of them as reality—only as fiction.

COOPER. I had the impression that in several of your novels and novellas, and in *The Pathseeker*[3] in particular, you address the question of the impossibility of mediating the past, or even the irretrievability of one's former self.

KERTÉSZ. Yes, one struggles to hang on to strands of the past, or to retrace them, but this struggle

---

3 Imre Kertész, *A nyomkereső. Két Regény* (Budapest: Szépirodalmi, 1977). Translated by Tim Wilkinson as *The Pathseeker* (New York: Melville House, 2008).

is doomed from the outset. The protagonist of *The Pathseeker* goes back, looks at the camp and tries to compose his memories but he feels estranged from everything he sees, even though it has determined his life and his search. One looks at the question of the loss of the Holocaust memory, and many authors have sought a form to express this loss. But *The Pathseeker*, I feel, is not solely about the memory of the Holocaust but, rather, about how one's past life is lost in the shadow of an overwhelming experience. One seeks in vain to identify with one's former self. The book went unnoticed when it was first published—there was not a single review. I had problems with the censors at the time, of course, with the dictatorship and its canon, an entirely artificial canon. It can be frustrating as a writer—one wonders whether what one has written is any good at all. I had the feeling I had wasted my energy. I'm lucky from this point of view because I was 60 when the regimes changed in Hungary. I still had enough energy to see things with a fresh eye and keep writing, books like *Liquidation*[4] and some collections of essays.

COOPER. You write in one of your essays that homeland is a term we should ponder. Herta Müller, the Bánát Schwab author who was awarded the Nobel Prize last year [2009], also writes with some suspicion and reservations about this term, *Heimat*.

KERTÉSZ. Well, her case is different. She fled Romania for Berlin during some of the worst years of Ceauseşcu's rule, whereas I decided to move here after the fall of Communism. I was moving, she was fleeing. And, of course, her situation in Romania was not the same either, as a German-speaker. It's not hard to understand that, in her case, 'homeland' is associated with negative experiences.

COOPER. And in yours?

KERTÉSZ. Honestly I don't know what to do with this word. Where is my homeland, or home? There's an excellent Italian restaurant in Berlin—are you familiar with Berlin?

COOPER. Only parts of it, it's a huge city.

---

4 Imre Kertész, *Felszámolás* (Budapest: Magvető, 2003). Translated by Tim Wilkinson as *Liquidation* (New York: Knopf, 2004).

KERTÉSZ. Near the König Hotel, in the villa quarter, there's an Italian restaurant run by two old Italian men. They're very friendly, they greet you with an embrace and a kiss on the lips. The word *Heimat* came up once and one of them said, 'I've lived in Germany for 40 years, I was born in Sicily but I've lived here for 40 years, and I feel at home here. What if I had been born on a train? Would the train be my homeland?' It's an artificial word. This doesn't mean that I don't love my homeland—I just don't know where it is, Hungary or Germany. Americans say home is where you hang your hat. I love that saying, that's how I feel.

COOPER. In your acceptance speech you mentioned the importance of the Hungarian language to you and how moving it was to be able to speak in Hungarian before a global audience. And you have often written on Sándor Márai, another Hungarian who lived away from Hungary but always wrote in Hungarian.

KERTÉSZ. Yes, he is something of an inspiration for me. He was a great fan of Thomas Mann, and Mann was another author who left the country of his birth. When they asked him in the United States about how he related to German culture, now that he had stepped out of it himself, he said, 'Wherever I am, German culture is there too.' This is a beautiful sentiment, and there is truth to it. Márai's case is a bit different, since the bourgeoisie in Hungary was never as strong as it was in Germany. His departure was a major loss to the country's already small bourgeoisie. It symbolized the flight of the bourgeoisie from Hungary. But he continued to write in Hungarian till the end.

COOPER. If you'll permit me one last question. In *Valaki más: A változás kronikája* (I–Another: Chronicle of a Metamorphosis)[5] you wrote that one cannot experience freedom in the place where one has lived in captivity. Is this why you decided to leave Budapest for Berlin?

KERTÉSZ. It's more complicated than that. I thought very seriously about leaving Hungary after the 1956 Revolution, but Budapest was where I had lived through two reigns of terror. I started to write about this, about my experiences of dictatorship, and I realized that I

5 Imre Kertész, *Valaki más: A Változás kronikája* (Budapest: Magvető, 1997).

didn't want to stop. And I didn't want to go where people didn't speak my mother tongue. I was 26 then. I couldn't learn a new language, write in a new language, at 26. Perhaps if I had left after the War . . . I had been in Buchenwald. It had been turned into a camp for displaced persons and I could have gone anywhere, Western Europe or the United States. But I had come back to Budapest. And at 26 it was too late. But I do not regret this. As I mentioned before, living under socialism was an inspiration even though a negative one. Those years gave me an insight into the degrading processes of and compromises made for survival. But once the Kádár regime fell, my fate no longer seemed tied to the city. Budapest was the scene of so many changes, war, occupation, revolution and every day scraping by.

But now it's a free city. That chapter of the past is closed. There is nothing that ties me to it any more. It's moving in new directions, and these directions have little to do with me.

THE HOLOCAUST AS CULTURE

When I came to Vienna for the first time in my life, three years ago, in 1989, I found myself in one of the picturesque squares of the inner city, from which stairs lead down to the Danube and narrow, cobblestoned streets meander between the old shops and entranceways. The soothing cityscape was disturbed by a single, unusual detail: on the corner of one of the sloping lanes were policemen standing guard, wearing berets and armed with machine guns. I soon learnt that the Jewish community of Vienna had its offices in a building nearby, next to which was the synagogue. About 50 years have passed since I last—back in my student days—attended a Jewish service. Suddenly I felt the urge to do so. At the entrance to the synagogue, however, they blocked my way. Two strapping young men wearing embroidered

This essay is the text of an address delivered on 23 October 1992 as part of the Jean Améry Symposium at the University of Vienna.

round caps inquired as to my intentions. It was no simple matter to enter. A few years ago there had been an attack at the synagogue, hence the policemen. Why did I want to go in, and who was I, they wanted to know. I told them I was a Hungarian author who, in some measure, had touched on the question of Jewish existence in his writings. Could I prove it, they asked. I could not. Say something in Hebrew. Not a single Hebrew word came to mind. But at least I knew, they continued the interrogation, what today was? It was not I who gave the answer but the Austrian lady, blonde, Catholic, accompanying me: Friday afternoon, the eve of the Sabbath. Finally, after much ado, they let us in.

Today I stand before you, ladies and gentlemen, every bit as irrelevant, unrecognized, every bit as much a stranger here as I was then at the gateway to the synagogue in Vienna. I speak before an audience that can hardly know my writings. I should perhaps begin with a bit of an explanation, reveal my qualifications, prove that I do indeed possess the exceedingly questionable privilege of speaking in public about Jean Améry and about existence as it has been branded by the Holocaust. Yet I do not mind this irrelevance at all. Indeed, it is precisely in this irrelevance that I think I may glimpse the possibility, today ever-dwindling, of making a statement at all. This irrelevance is the emblem of an entangled, transitional and unrecognized situation in which a survivor such as Améry is compelled to exist so that his existence can come forth and find expression as fate, whether in a tragic gesture, as in his case, or otherwise. The Holocaust has its saints, like any subculture; and if the living memory of the events survives then it will survive not because of the official orations but, rather, through the lives of those who bore evidence.

With this I have provided a rough sketch of the subject on which I wish to say a few words to you. From the first moment, when it had not yet become known to the wider world but, rather, unfolded day by day in the hidden recesses of nameless, obscure places and was the secret of the accomplices, victims and henchmen, from that first moment the Holocaust brought with it a horrible dread—a dread that it might be forgotten. This dread was greater than the horrors, than the individual lives and deaths, than the avid demand for justice. It was 'beyond guilt and atonement',[1]

---

1 The German title of Améry's work is *Jenseits Von Schuld Und Sühne: Bewältigungsversuche Eines Überwältigen* (Munich: Szczesny, 1966). The title of the English translation, *At the Mind's*

to quote the title of Améry's book, a book about which we are all speaking here today. From the very beginning, this dread was pervaded by a kind of metaphysical feeling characteristic of religions, of religious sentiments. And perhaps the phrase from the Bible is the most fitting here: 'The voice of thy brother's blood crieth unto me from the ground.' If a moment ago I referred to the Holocaust as a subculture, meaning a spiritual and emotional community bound by a certain cult-like mentality, I took as my point of departure this passionate resistance against forgetting, this demand which has, over time, increased. Whether the broader culture recognizes this demand, even accepts and espouses it, depends on the extent to which this demand proves justified.

And lo, our words have already channelled us, unawares, into a particular context. We used the word subculture, and this word we connected with the global consciousness or, more precisely,

Limits: Contemplations by a Survivor on Auschwitz and its Realities (Sidney Rosenfeld and Stella P. Rosenfeld trans) (Bloomington and Indianapolis: Indiana University Press, 2009) is taken from the title of the first essay in the collection. The original German title is an allusion to Nietzsche's Jenseits von Gut und Böse (Beyond Good and Evil) (1886) and Dostoyevsky's Crime and Punishment (1866) in English and Schuld und Sühne in commonly used German translations.

with the Euro-American civilization to which, in the end, all of us who have gathered here to speak of Améry belong. But what does this have to do with the lonely exile, the stranger, the man branded and condemned, the man who had every individual's birthright, his 'trust in the world' (*Weltvertrauen*), thrashed out of him with a horse-whip? In the first chapter of his book,[2] Améry radically calls to account intellectual history as well as the 'intellectual', the embodiment of this history. 'Reduced to its most concise form,' he writes, 'the question that arises is: Did intellectual background and an intellectual basic disposition help a camp prisoner in the decisive moments? Did they make survival easier for him?'[3] Améry's radical answer is: No. No, because, among other reasons, 'the spiritual and aesthetic heritage had passed over into the uncontested and uncontestable ownership of the enemy.'[4] 'In Auschwitz [. . .] the isolated individual had to relinquish all of German culture, including [Albrecht] Dürer and [Johann Maximilian] Reger, Andreas Gryphius and Georg

2 Améry, 'At the Mind's Limits' in *At the Mind's Limits*, pp. 1–20.
3 Ibid., p. 5.
4 Ibid., p. 8.

Trakl, to even the lowest SS man.'[5] The situation
of the intellectual was definitely made more difficult by the knowledge of culture, writes Améry,
though the most ponderous and haunting temp-
tation of reflection—into which the intellectual
could be led by his historical consciousness and
his knowledge of culture—was self-denial: What
if the enemy is right? For is power not always
right? And the power of the SS towered so 'mon-
strously' and so 'indomitably' over the prisoner in
Auschwitz that in the end he might have found its
logic 'reasonable'.

These are unavoidable thoughts, my esteemed
audience. Every prisoner in Auschwitz who did not
depend on some religious, racial or political ideal,
who had no faith, no people and no higher calling,
only his or her fate, his or her mere existence, every
lonely intellectual raised these questions. Each of
them drew up an indictment of culture. Hegel's
contention that reason is universal proved a grave
error, just as culture too is not universal. Culture
is privileged consciousness, and this consciousness objectifies, and the right to objectify is the
possession of the privileged consciousness. Hence

---

5 Ibid.

the terrible dread that culture would expunge from itself all knowledge of the Holocaust, of Auschwitz. 'You know how much I used to like Plato? Today I realize he lied,' writes another Auschwitz prisoner, the Polish Catholic Borowski, in one of his immortal narratives.[6] 'For the things of this world are not a reflection of the ideal, but a product of human sweat, blood, and hard labour.'[7] 'If the Germans win the war, what will the world know about us?'

> They will kill off our families, our sick, our aged. They will murder our children. And we shall be forgotten, drowned out by the voices of the poets, the jurists, the philosophers, the priests. They will produce their own beauty, virtue, and truth. They will produce religion.[8]

This was echoed 20 years later in the words of Améry:

---

6 Kertész is referring to *Pożegnanie z Marią* (Farewell to Maria) (Warsaw: Wiedza, 1948), a collection of short stories by Tadeusz Borowski. The English translation by Barbara Vedder is named after the story 'Prosz pa stwa do gazu' (*This Way for the Gas, Ladies and Gentlemen*, London: Penguin, 1976).

7 Borowski, 'Auschwitz, Our Home (A Letter)' in *This Way for the Gas*, pp. 132–3.

8 Ibid., p. 132.

All recognizable signs suggest that natural time will reject the moral demands of
our resentment and finally extinguish
them [. . .] We, the victims, will appear as
the truly incorrigible, irreconcilable ones,
as the anti-historical reactionaries in the
exact sense of the word, and in the end it
will seem like a technical mishap that
some of us still survived.[9]

As I say, these thoughts are unavoidable. What
could be more foolish than to resist them, to
debate or to qualify them? It is the situation that
needs to be qualified, the situation that compels us
to conceive of and reflect on such thoughts. Only
then will we ascertain that they are not unavoidable
but well founded and entirely justified.

On the other hand, it should not escape our
notice that these thoughts and the form in which
they appear are in the end manifestations of culture, indeed, products of culture. Améry turns to
the very intellectual heritage he disavowed. He was
too clever to attempt to conceal this paradox. Even
the title of the book about which we are speaking
today, *Jenseits von Schuld und Sühne*, is an allusion

9 Améry, *At the Mind's Limits*, p. 80.

both to Nietzsche and Dostoyevsky. One of his books is titled *Unmeisterliche Wanderjahre* (1971), calling directly on Goethe, through the reference to *Wilhelm Meisters' Wanderjahre* (1821), to give testimony. His language is the finest literary German, his razor-sharp style chiselled from the French essay. Though that intellect was of no assistance to him in Auschwitz, he had to call that very same intellect to his aid in order to formulate his indictment against Auschwitz. He found no way out of culture. He went from culture to Auschwitz and then from Auschwitz back to culture, as if from one camp to the other, and the language and intellectual world of culture enclosed him like the barbed-wire fence of Auschwitz. He survived Auschwitz; and if he wished to survive his survival, if he wanted to invest it with some meaning, or rather content, then, as a writer, he was compelled to see that the only chance to do so lay in self-documentation, self-examination, objectification, in other words, culture. 'Like a dog!—he said, it was as if the shame would outlive him.'[10] But in order to survive he had to formulate his shame deftly and give what he had formulated lasting

10 Franz Kafka, *The Trial* (Idris Parry trans.) (London: Penguin, 2007), p. 178.

form. In other words, he had to become a good writer.

We can ponder this paradox interminably. If he wanted to rise up against transience, amoral time, then he had to stake his life on writing until, eventually, he flung life aside as well. Whether or not his suicide belongs to his *oeuvre* is another question, one on which we will touch only timidly and in passing. 'In seiner Niederlage findet der Gläubige seinen Sieg,' writes Kierkegaard: 'In his defeat the man of faith finds his victory.' The subtitle of Améry's book is even more telling: *Bewältigungsversuche eines Überwältigten*, which may be roughly translated as 'Attempts at Empowerment by a Person Overpowered'. But how can a writer be empowered? Does he take power? In a certain sense, yes, he does. I mentioned that the right to objectify is the right, one could say even the power, of the privileged. The man branded and condemned to die, whom this power has trodden underfoot, now takes back the right to objectify. Perhaps this thought lies hidden in the depths of 'Resentments', that famous chapter of his book. In a novel by another Auschwitz survivor, we find the following lines:

I can discern only one possible explanation for my stubborn passion: maybe I had started writing in order to gain my revenge on the world. To gain revenge and regain from it what it had robbed me of. Perhaps my adrenal glands, which I managed to preserve intact even from Auschwitz, are hypersecretors of adrenaline. Why not? After all, representation contains an innate power in which the aggressive instinct can subside for a moment and produce an equipoise, a temporary respite. Maybe that is what I wanted. Yes, to grab hold, if only in my imagination and by artistic means, of the reality that all too really holds me in its power; to subjectivize my perpetual objectivity, to become the name-giver instead of the named.[11]

(That Auschwitz survivor is standing here before you, and the title of the novel is *A kudarc* and when I wrote these lines I had never even heard of Jean Améry.)

---

11 Kertész, *The Fiasco*, p. 93.

In the chapter entitled 'Torture', Améry takes a stand against the classification 'totalitarianism' which blurs together all forms of party dictatorship, in particular those of Hitler and Stalin. He takes a stand against the notion that it was not Hitler who was the executioner but that it was the sort of vague notion called 'totatlitarianism'. Remaining cautious not to steer my comments, even accidentally, in the direction of a political essay, I would like to note that I have a profound understanding of Améry's distinction. A person tortured, who bears the weight and consequences of the fate he has shouldered, is not willing to negotiate with a general principle. What would become of his freedom? His fate? His personality? Furthermore, with whom should he settle accounts, towards whom should he feel and assert his 'resentment', if everything is as intelligible, simple, and impersonal as the abstract notion of totalitarianism? Améry found himself confronted with people, 'anti-people' (*Gegenmenschen*); it was not totalitarianism that beat him with a horsewhip and hung him by his shackled wrists but Lieutenant Praust, who happened to speak a Berlin dialect.

In addition, however they might have classified him—or perhaps he did so himself. He was, first and foremost, a German writer and philosopher, and in his mind the outrage was, first and foremost, German Nazism. Russian Bolshevism most certainly ranked second. This is logical—indeed, no one could seriously put an equal sign between the two. 'I am convinced,' writes Améry, 'beyond all personal experiences, that torture was not an accidental quality of this Third Reich but its essence.'[12] We should note, however, that torture was not an accidental quality of the hammer-and-sickle totalitarian state either but its essence as well. Torture is, in most cases, the essence of every absolute raised to the level of the state, every dictatorship that swells power to autocracy. Améry acknowledges this.

On some other questions, however, he seems to be a bit mulish. He is capable, for instance, of speaking of anti-Semitism as if the prejudice were today what it was in the time of our grandfathers. Yet this is precisely what the Nazis wanted the people to believe—precisely what anyone who follows the Nazis today, whether in Eastern or Western Europe or elsewhere in the world, wants the people to believe. It is our duty, however, to recognize the

---

12 Améry, *At the Mind's Limits*, p. 24.

qualitative difference. Nineteenth-century anti-Semitism would hardly have been able, or have wanted, to conceive of the *Endlösung*. Auschwitz cannot be explained with reference to the ideas of common, archaic, dare I say classical?, anti-Semitism—this we must understand very clearly. There is no organic connection between the two. Our age is not the age of anti-Semitism but of Auschwitz. And the anti-Semite of our age no longer spurns Jews; rather, he longs for Auschwitz. At his trial in Jerusalem, Eichmann confessed that he had never been an anti-Semite. And while the audience burst into laughter at these words, I by no means considered it impossible that he was telling the truth. In order to murder millions of Jews, the totalitarian state needs not anti-Semites but good organizers. We must be clear: no totalitarian party or state can exist without discrimination, and the totalitarian form of discrimination is necessarily mass murder.

I had to take this detour in order to return to what Améry characterized with such painful precision as a 'technical mishap'. No one could have felt more profoundly the nature of his existence as the incidental consequence of a technical mishap than a person, overpowered simply by virtue of being a Jew, who tried to carry out his or her attempts at empowerment under a so-called socialism. The dictatorship of the proletariat did not like people to speak of the Holocaust. It silenced all such voices or forced them into schemas of conformist euphemisms. If one were nonetheless bold enough to entertain the notion that Auschwitz was, after the Crucifixion, the most significant event for humankind which had traumatically fallen, so to speak, through European ethical culture, and if one were to wish to approach these questions with the appropriate seriousness, then one could count on being condemned from the outset to complete solitude and isolation. One could assume that one's books would be printed in limited numbers, if at all, and one could be confident of being banished to the margins of literary and intellectual life, thrust into the silence of official critical opinion, much like solitary confinement. In other words, once sentenced to death himself, the author could now expect the same sentence to be passed over his work.

There are, of course, perfectly good reasons, and not particularly enigmatic ones, to explain why hammer-and-sickle totalitarianism identified itself, with regard to the Holocaust, with Swastika totalitarianism. I would, however, prefer to speak instead of the uses this had. I have recently been thinking about how the Holocaust claimed its victims not only at that time and in the concentration camps but also elsewhere, decades later. As if the liberation of the camps merely deferred the sentences which were later carried out by the condemned themselves. Celan, Borowski and Améry all committed suicide, even Primo Levi who, in one of his polemical essays, opposed Améry's resolute existential radicalism. If from time to time I compare these fates, demonstrative in many senses, with my own, then I am forced to conclude that clearly I was helped over the course of the past decades by a 'society' that, following Auschwitz, amply demonstrated through the form of so-called Stalinism that there could be no question of freedom, liberation, catharsis, etc.—none of the things intellectuals and philosophers in more fortunate climes not only spoke of but also clearly believed in. I was trapped in a society that guaranteed me the continued life of a prisoner, thereby also excluding the possibility of my erring. This is clearly why I was not engulfed by the high tide of disappointments that overwhelmed those who had similar experiences but who found themselves living in more open societies, the rising waters first splashing at their feet as they tried to flee, then slowly rising to their throats. And as I was not the only prisoner—rather, the nation in which I lived was imprisoned as well—I did not have any problem of identity.

Now that the walls of the prison have fallen, one can hear again, in the cacophony among the ruins, the hoarse cry of post-Auschwitz anti-Semitism, in other words an anti-Semitism that looks with approval on Auschwitz. Like the hero of Camus's *The Stranger* (1942), I greet the cries of hatred as brotherly voices. I am not afraid—the Holocaust turned any fear of anti-Semites in me to ash. What does it have to do with me? Programmatic anti-Semitism after Auschwitz is a private affair that might well liquidate me even today but that would be little more than a bold anachronism, a blunder or a lapse in which, as Hegel may have said say, there would be little trace of the *Weltgeist*. It would be provincial, it would show lack of cultivation. 'Entirely a matter for the anti-Semites, their disgrace or their sickness,'[13] as Améry himself wrote. However, it does at least awaken me again to my actual situation in case the fleeting

---

13 Ibid., p. 92.

illusion of my freedom regained made me forget it for a passing moment.

This condition in and of itself does not merit much attention. It is the condition of a survivor who has tried to survive his survival and, what is more, interpret it; who as a member of the last generation of survivors is well aware that as this generation vanishes from this world, so too will the living memory of the Holocaust. His presence here is a technical mishap, an accident, which continuously begs some justification although it is in fact unjustifiable. But does not this condition seem a reminiscent of the general and cosmic condition of humankind as we have come to know it through the interpretation of modern philosophy and anthropology? Whenever he writes of his alienation, his loss of 'faith in the world', his social loneliness and existential exile, Améry in my view goes beyond the narrowly defined framework of his book and addresses, quite simply, the human condition. The survivor is merely the tragic bearer of the human condition of the era, one who has experienced and endured Auschwitz, the apogee of that condition, its presence looming over the horizon behind us like the horrific vision of a deranged mind; and though increasingly distant, its outline, far from dwindling, seems clearer, stronger. It is quite apparent today that survival is not the personal problem of those who remained. The long, dark shadow of the Holocaust spreads over the whole of the civilization in which it took place, a civilization which must now live with the burden and the consequences of what happened.

You could say that I exaggerate, for you barely come across traces of these consequences. The world has been speaking of other things for some time now. This, however, is merely the surface, merely appearance. As long as they are vital, the questions are important. And if we examine whether the question of the Holocaust is a vital question for European civilization, European consciousness, then we find that the answer is yes. Because the very civilization within the frameworks of which the Holocaust occurred must reflect on it. Otherwise it too will become a civilization of accident and mishap, no more than a debilitated organism drifting helplessly towards annihilation. It cannot avoid arriving at a decision.

But what am I saying?—it appears already to have reached a decision. Améry's and Borowski's fear—that in the end the murderers would be in the right—seems to have been unfounded. State-sponsored genocide, the annihilation of a people, today and for the foreseeable future is no culture in Europe—only a practice. This practice, however, is indefensible; and if it were suddenly to become morally justifiable, then this would mean the end of life. Everyone is clear on this. A whole host of works in history and the social sciences has attempted to 'work through' the Holocaust. Widely diverging interpretations have been given, from the banality of evil to demonological works. I even read in the works of one philosopher that the Holocaust does not fit into history, as if history were some sort of chest of drawers whose size would determine what fit and what did not. She was unquestionably correct in one respect, however: the Holocaust was not, in its essence, a historical event. Just like the Lord handing over the inscribed tablets of stone to Moses on Mount Sinai was not a historical event.

I am not entirely sure that the outlines of what I have been trying to say have emerged clearly. Yet I have been speaking of a single question from the very beginning, a question that it is not customary and perhaps not terribly polite to raise openly although it is a question which must be resolved in accordance with the same mysterious and lengthy process through which all great ethical questions are. And the question is this: Can the Holocaust give rise to values? In my view, the process that has been underway for decades has now arrived at— and indeed is grappling with—precisely this question, a question that was at first stifled and then documented. This, however, proved insufficient. For as I said, the question must be resolved, and this means passing a value judgement. As Santayana said, one who does not remember history is bound to live through it again. A viable society must maintain and continuously renew its knowledge and awareness of itself and its conditions. And if we decide that the grave, black memorial service of the Holocaust is an indispensable part of this awareness, then this decision must be based not on some notion of compassion or contrition but on a living value judgement. The Holocaust is a value, because through immeasurable sufferings it has led to immeasurable knowledge, and thereby contains immeasurable moral reserves.

If preserved, the tragic insight into the world of the morality that survived the Holocaust may yet enrich European consciousness, now beset with crisis, much as the Greek genius, faced with barbarism and fighting the Persian War, created the antique tragedies that serve as an eternal model. If the Holocaust today has created a culture, as it undeniably has and continues to do, its literature may draw inspiration from the two sources of European culture, the Bible and Greek tragedy, so that irredeemable reality may give rise to redemption: the spirit, catharsis.

It's quite possible that you consider much of what I have said to be a bit Utopian—one sees, after all, no trace of this in the real world. Indeed, in the real world one sees quite the opposite: indifferent masses, cynical ideologies, amnesia, massacres, chaos and confusion. But significant events are not always captured clearly in the mirror of the realities of the present moment. And I am speaking, moreover, of a process the outlines of which I think I have discerned but the outcome of which, of course, I cannot know. As I said at the very beginning, we live in the context of a culture, and in this context the dead body of Jean Améry is to be found in the monument—still under construction—to the Holocaust, where he himself laid it down, like a blood-soaked flower.

Imre Kertész, 1992